Digging up our Past

The Archaeological Excavations in Old College Quad

Jean Grier and Mary Bownes
© The University of Edinburgh, 2016

ISBN 978-0-9534945-4-5

Published by the University of Edinburgh Communications and Public Affairs

Introduction

Old College – the heart of the University of Edinburgh

Old College has been the heart of the University of Edinburgh for around 200 years. The University itself is much older – it was founded in 1583 as the Tounis College or 'town's college'. For the next 200 years, the college operated in an assortment of buildings on the site of what is now Old College. Towards the end of the 18th century, with the University growing in status and expanding in student numbers, new purpose-built premises were called for and a competition was held to design them. Architect Robert Adam won the competition, and work started on the new buildings in 1789. Building didn't proceed smoothly and it was many decades before work was completed. William Playfair won a later competition to complete the project in 1816, though in fact he changed the plans a lot. The central quadrangle or 'quad' was used over the years for delivery carts and later as a car park, a boring expanse of grey gravel which did nothing to set off the fine buildings surrounding the quad, and so the University was delighted to receive a very generous private donation in 2010 specifically to enhance the quad.

The archaeological dig

Prior to laying the new paving stones, we carried out an archaeological dig – and this revealed a staggering amount of information about the early years of the University, and indeed of the city we are part of. This short guide will lead you around the quad as we uncover our past and give you a glimpse of our long and fascinating history. So join us on a journey through space and time using the typical findings of an archaeological dig – uncovering some things we all predicted would be there and others things which were unexpected. For an academic institution it is exciting to dig into our past and we hope that you will be fascinated too as we uncover not just building remains but artefacts that tell us about how people lived, how chemistry was studied during the Scottish Enlightenment, and much more.

As is often the case with big projects, completing the dig and completing the resurfacing of the quad on time was a fine balancing act, involving many people. We worked with the City Archaeologist's advice throughout – the dig was part of the Council's planning requirements for the whole quad project – and the finds will eventually be curated by the Council at the Museum of Edinburgh.

South West Corner of the New University, with Part of the Old Buildings South College Street and Drummond Street.

Why was a dig useful?

One might think that with all that has been written and investigated about the University and the city and its history there would be nothing left to discover from an archaeological dig. However, techniques have moved on a lot over the years and having access to human bones, for example, can now reveal so much information about whether people were well-nourished, what sort of illnesses they might have had during their lives, what sort of jobs they may have done, how they died and how old they were when they died. We can find out about the materials used for buildings, the techniques employed and perhaps where materials came from. Interestingly we can find out about how people were connected across the nation and beyond by these materials and techniques. The chemistry finds are especially revealing in this area.

Perhaps the most unexpected thing is that although there are many drawings of the city and the area around the University over time, it is hard to know how things really looked and how the buildings juxtaposed. 'Artistic licence' is a phrase often used, and there was much freedom on the part of the artist to move things a bit or change their proportions to make them look better. And sometimes – like the modern 'concept drawings' done by architects today – pictures may have been used to give an impression of what was intended rather than being an accurate plan of what was actually built. Of course, mistakes were also made, and after two hundred years or more, a lot of detective work may be needed to uncover the true position.

To illustrate what the dig might be able to establish, look at the two images below. They are almost like a 'spot the difference' quiz. The basic layout and many of the buildings are the same, but look more closely and there are several differences. Most significantly, perhaps, one caption calls this the 'South West Corner' and the other calls it the 'South East Corner'. Clearly, something is wrong. Once buildings have been demolished, it may be impossible to know for certain what they looked like – but the archaeology can often pinpoint the exact location of where they stood, and so help our understanding of the site as a whole.

South East Corner of the New University with Part of the Old Buildings, South College Street, and Drummond Street.

The Dig Process

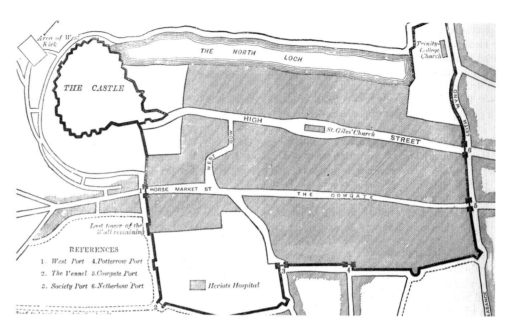

An archaeological dig doesn't proceed in a chronologically logical order. Usually, the newest stuff is the first to be uncovered, but if a site is very 'messy' – with lots of work having gone on over centuries – old material may be mixed in with newer materials, or with even older material. Disentangling this can be difficult – and so in this book we'll work our way around the quad and look at the areas we unearthed in turn.

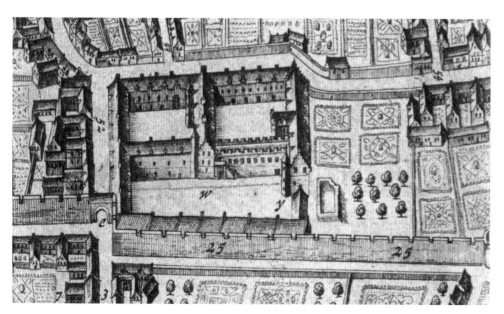

Old maps and drawings are a good starting point for research, though they are rarely very accurate.

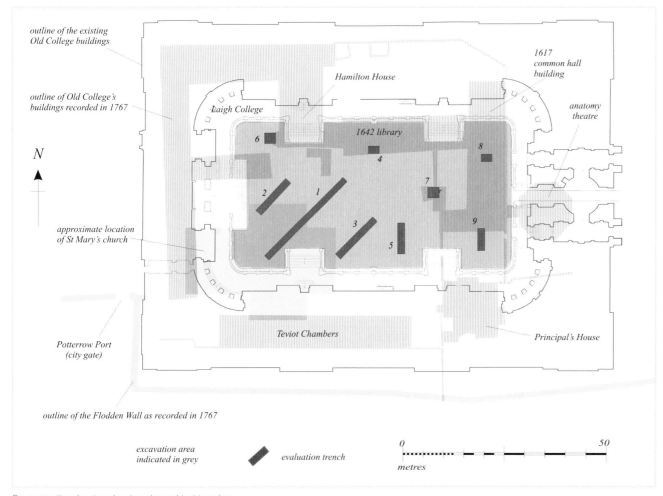

outline of the existing Old College buildings

outline of Old College's buildings recorded in 1767

Laigh College

Hamilton House

1642 library

1617 common hall building

anatomy theatre

N
▲

6

4

8

7

2   1

3

9

5

approximate location of St Mary's church

Potterrow Port (city gate)

Teviot Chambers

Principal's House

outline of the Flodden Wall as recorded in 1767

excavation area indicated in grey   ▬ evaluation trench

0   50

metres

Pre-excavation drawing showing planned test trenches.

The dig turned up a variety of small finds, including coins, stoppers, cutlery and flasks for chemicals.

This elegant fragment of lustred glass was probably from a fine drinking vessel.

Before starting properly on any excavations, archaeologists do a lot of desk-based research. What do we know about the site? What might we find? Where might we find it? Old maps and drawings aren't always accurate, so the next stage is to dig some test trenches – or 'sondages', to use their technical name. These may reveal hidden walls or foundations, allowing us to pinpoint a feature more accurately. They show us how deep we need to go to find what we are looking for. They may produce 'small finds' – buttons, coins, broken pottery – which help us date the area we are digging in. Even seemingly trivial finds like tiny pieces of charcoal, burnt grains or broken oyster shells can tell us about human occupation – about the position of a hearth, or about what people were eating. And sometimes the test trenches produce nothing at all!

For the purposes of the excavation, the quad was divided into six equal-sized areas. This map shows where the test trenches were cut.

Informed by what the test trenches revealed, the process of digging the site then proceeds. But even once the digging is over, the archaeologists' work is not complete. Months of analysis and further research can go on after a dig – and we'll learn about some of the post-excavation information we've gleaned as we work our way around the quad.

Gruesome Discoveries

The bulldozers moved in and cleared the gravel and top soil. The archaeologists had barely started digging when they came across graves and human remains very close to the surface near the middle of the quad. We were expecting to uncover skeletons – we knew there had been a churchyard in the area – but not quite so near the surface. Bodies were exposed in 45 graves; in other graves the bones had not survived. We were able to work out the sex of most of the skeletons from measurement of the bones – pelvis and skull differ in males and females, as does the size of the long bones.

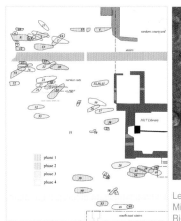

Left: Drawing showing the position of graves.
Middle: A well-preserved skeleton.
Right: One grave contained three skeletons - two adults and a child.

A general view of the entire site, showing some of the graves and clear evidence of the many drains uncovered.

Although the graves were body-shaped, in general there was no evidence of coffins being used. The people were clearly buried just in cloth shrouds as pins and copper wires to hold shrouds together were found in the graves. The absence of coffins suggests that these people were not wealthy. Nearly everyone was laid with their heads to the west and legs to the east, which is typical in Christian cemeteries, so that the dead can rise facing the rising sun on judgement day.

One grave containing three skeletons was especially interesting - two adults, who were buried holding hands, and a child of roughly nine years old. It's very unlikely we'll ever know who they were – perhaps a family who fell prey to one of the many outbreaks of Plague which occurred periodically.

Unfortunately many of the bones were badly damaged due to years of heavy vehicles driving over them and many graves had been damaged when the quad had been dug up over the years to lay drains at various points in the University's history. We excavated all the graves where exposed human remains were judged to be at risk of damage from subsequent construction works on the site.

Some interesting statistics:

Estimated stature of males 168 cm
(compared with just under 173 cm today)

Females 158 cm – rather similar to late medieval graves at St Giles Cathedral.
(The average height of women in Scotland today is 160 cm)

The work of the archaeologists continues long after the actual digging is completed, and laboratory analysis of the bones has revealed information about how these people lived – their illnesses and occupations.

The shape of the lower limbs often showed a flathead femur and tibia typical of walking long distances on rough ground and typical of pre-industrial peoples. There is evidence in the discs in the vertebrae of heavy lifting by the males. The eye sockets of several showed iron deficiency, and teeth showed some evidence of nutritional stress. In other words, these people had a hard life of physical labour, a relatively poor diet, and experienced times when there was just not enough food. Although some had fractured bones during their lives, these had healed and were not the cause of death.

Why were the burials so close to the surface? Sometimes it is only towards the end of a dig that information starts to make sense. These people had not been buried in shallow graves, but the site on which Old College is built was originally quite a sloping site, and much work was done to level it before the 'new' buildings were created. This took large quantities of earth from one end of the site to the other. It also made the site very 'messy' and difficult to interpret, with old material mixed in with newer material across the site.

Research is still being done on the bone samples, and in due course we may discover much more about these people. Were they born in the Edinburgh area, or did they move here as adults? Did they all have a similar diet, suggesting they were of similar social status, or were some wealthier than others? Did the average social status change over the time when the cemetery was in use? None of them were buried in coffins and all appear to have been buried in shrouds rather than clothes, suggesting that they were from similar social backgrounds, but we may learn more about this as research continues. As the burials were in a consecrated Christian cemetery, the remains will be reinterred in due course, though samples of bone and tooth will be retained for future research.

Hamilton House

Hamilton House was one of the first buildings to be excavated. What we found were steps linking Hamilton House to the Laigh College, the footings of various staircases, a kitchen fireplace and slop sink, and a lot of drains. This helped us to flesh out much of the otherwise scanty information we had about the University's first home.

Excavating the kitchen fireplace.

The stair footing.

Archaeological evidence revealed the remains of stairs which once would have connected High College Court to Laigh College. James Jossie oversaw much of the construction of Laigh College, which included the stair link, made between the two courts, between 1640 and 1644. Demolition deposits were found on top of Jossie's stairs, dating to around 1790, when Hamilton House was demolished.

As the archaeologists began to dig further into the remains of Hamilton House, a small area sectioned off by walls on either side was discovered. The charcoal, ash and soot found here indicated that the archaeologists had found the kitchen fireplace! This fireplace's use was short lived and it was later filled in, which suggests that this particular room was not always used as a kitchen area and perhaps was eventually used as storage space.

Hamilton House was a mansion which had been built in 1552 for the Duke of Chatelherault and 2nd Earl of Arran, James Hamilton. He was cousin to Mary, Queen of Scots and was a wealthy, well-connected man. Although no detailed pictures of Hamilton House can be found, the Duke also owned Kinneill House near Bo'ness in West Lothian. Kinneill has some fine panelling and some wonderful painted ceilings; perhaps Hamilton House did too.

James Hamilton got on the wrong side of the authorities in some of the political wrangling which went on in Scotland in the sixteenth century, and as a result of which he had to forfeit Hamilton House – and the rest of the estate around it – to the Crown in 1571. The Crown later sold the property to the town council for £1,000. The council housed the new college at this location – though Hamilton's descendants later sued the council for the value of the property, settling the dispute for £3,000 – and in due course, the college bought or built other buildings around the site.

Further investigation revealed that there were two phases to the construction of Hamilton House. The earlier phase was the construction of the main body of the building. The following phase consisted of the addition of a chamber, a passage which would have allowed another entrance to Hamilton House, and a stair tower which is also evident in textual evidence as described by John Laurie in 1767.

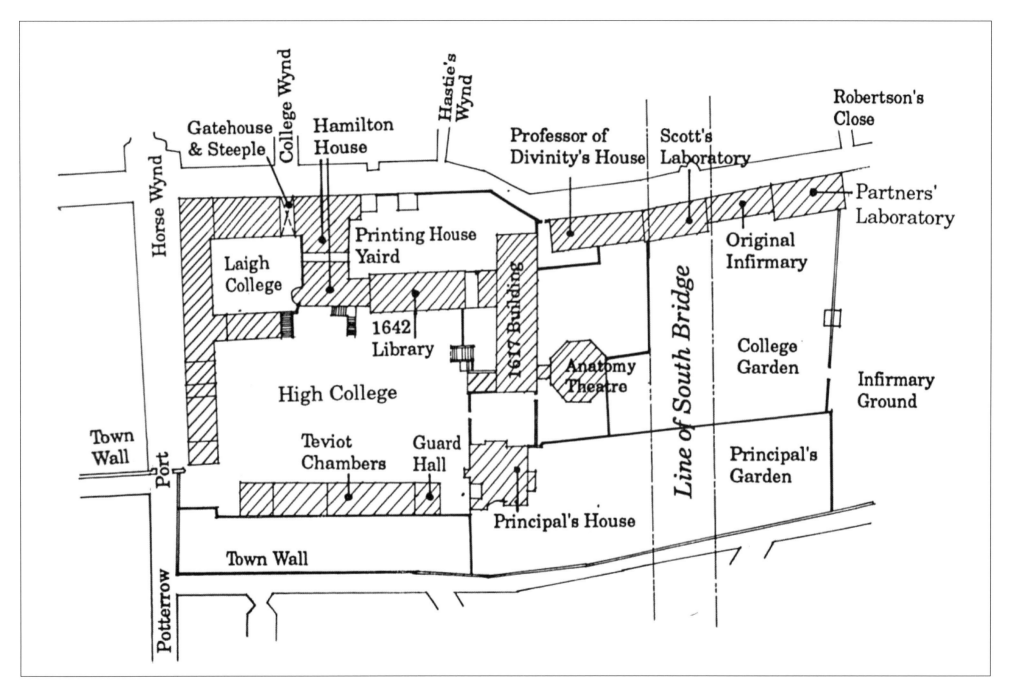

The buildings of the college, later cut through by South Bridge, from *The Building of Old College,* Fraser.

The Old Library or 1642 Library

Although it was referred to as 'the old library', 'old' is a relative term! In fact, this building was the second major library to be built on the Old College site, and arguably the third library the University had developed – Clement Litil had given his collection of books to form a library before the University even existed. Soon after the Tounis College was founded, the books were transferred to a room in Hamilton House, and later to the 1617 building. There are many references in council records to problems with the library, which suffered from 'moustyness' and a roof which leaked far too often. Although a special grant was allocated to buy coal to warm the room and presumably dispel the moustyness, the books were clearly being damaged. So in 1642, an act was made for building a 'new library'.

The deposits in Sondage 4 revealed a complex and confusing story. However, with reference to the remains available and textual evidence, archaeologists concluded that in this one trench there was the interior of Hamilton House and the interior of the 1642 library. Thomas Craufurd, Professor of Philosophy and Mathematics, wrote a history of the University from 1580 to 1646. It is very valuable to archaeologists as Craufurd, writing in 1646, was describing developments which were within living memory, which then means that archaeological evidence concerning construction found during the excavation can be verified confidently.

What Craufurd said about the building of the 1642 Library was that a number of chambers were built at this time. He used a technical term – 'jamb' – to refer to the wing of a building, and explained that the library ran 'from the south jamb of the old house to the jamb of the great hall' and had a lead-covered roof. He also said that '...a considerable number of honest and bountiful citizens' wanted to continue building along the west wall 'as far almost as the latrines, and from thence eastward to the Provost's lodging' but the costs proved too high. Plans were clearly scaled back, with just two chambers 'in the corner besouth James Moray's chambers, with the cellar beneath' being added, two more built by Archibald Sydserf, Bailie, and 'the two high chambers betwext the corner chambers and Sir Thomas Hope's' – a total of six chambers added.

In 1644 a series of civil wars unsettled the town, and an outbreak of plague in 1645 saw the whole University decamped to Linlithgow for a year, where the 'Great Kirk' was fitted out to provide for the students. The absence of the students perhaps enabled building work to carry on apace in Edinburgh during this time, with more chambers being added. There is evidence of this during the excavation with deposits which clearly indicate construction taking place in High College Court and Laigh Court between the years of 1640 -1644.

Bookplate from one of the books donated by Clement Litil in 1580.

The 1642 Library on the left, with the library above and the hall below; the building at right-angles to it is the 1617 building.

Museum, Hall, Library

College 1817.—

Chemistry and Professor Joseph Black

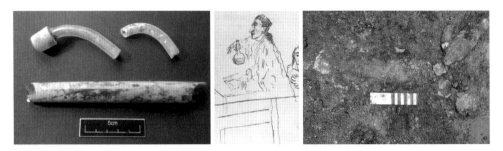

From left to right: After excavation, small finds are carefully cleaned and recorded.
Then, as now, students doodled in their notebooks. Here is Professor Black in class.
Various brightly-coloured deposits in the soil alerted archaeologists to the presence of toxic chemicals.

As the dig moved around the quad, we expected to find evidence of the chemistry teaching and research which happened in the late 1700s. Evidence there was in the way of some rather alarming chemicals found in the occupation deposits of the 1642 library cellar. The archaeologists quickly had to don protective clothing to continue their excavations. They found many nasty chemicals which are highly toxic even after years buried in the ground… The brightly coloured red and pink compounds were later identified to contain mercury, arsenic and cobalt. The site needed to be decontaminated before the dig could continue; of course at the time these chemicals were left there people had no idea how dangerous they were. There were no health and safety procedures, so teachers and students just threw stuff out after their teaching demonstrations and experiments.

From left to right: A more formal portrait of Joseph Black, whose lectures were well attended.
Any small items found are initially put into a plastic tray and their positions noted before formal identification and careful cleaning.

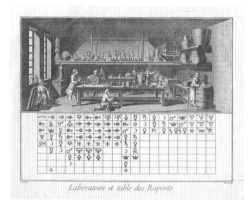

Laboratoire et table des Raports

Top: Joseph Black's chemistry laboratory.

Middle: Members of the public also attended lectures given by some of the more flamboyant professors.

Bottom: Students were issued with cards allowing them access to lectures; this card allows William Dean to attend Professor Black's classes in 1769.

Chemicals can still be highly toxic years after being buried.

Joseph Black was an exceptional Enlightenment scientist born in April 1728. He graduated as an MD (Doctor of Medicine) in Edinburgh but he had already been studying chemistry in Glasgow with William Cullen. In 1756 he prepared a paper showing that materials such as magnesium carbonate contained a gas which he called 'fixed air' and which we now know as carbon dioxide. This was the beginning of a revolution in chemistry and Black was central to it.

Joseph Black developed and created a balance using a beam of fir wood resting on a needle over a small brass holder. Using this he could accurately measure very small weights, probably down to 0.05mg.

Eventually, after doing much research in Glasgow and teaching there, he gained a chair in Edinburgh after the retirement of his previous mentor, William Cullen. Black was an excellent teacher and helped develop the whole discipline of chemistry at Edinburgh. Black not only discovered carbon dioxide, but magnesium, specific heat and latent heat. He did wonderful experiments in front of his class to illustrate the work he was doing, and in the 1790s over 200 students would attend his lectures. In 1800, a gallery had to be added to his classroom to increase capacity, and further enlargements were made just two years later. As Black's health declined, Thomas Hope – another very influential chemist – took over from him.

The 1617 Building

The absence of any room big enough to accommodate all the students for daily meetings or prayers was a limitation, and laureation ceremonies had to be held in churches in the town. 'Laureations' were effectively graduation ceremonies, and involved a process whereby the students were asked questions – in Latin – and made their responses, all done in public. That would be a very daunting experience for students today and it is likely it was just as stressful then.

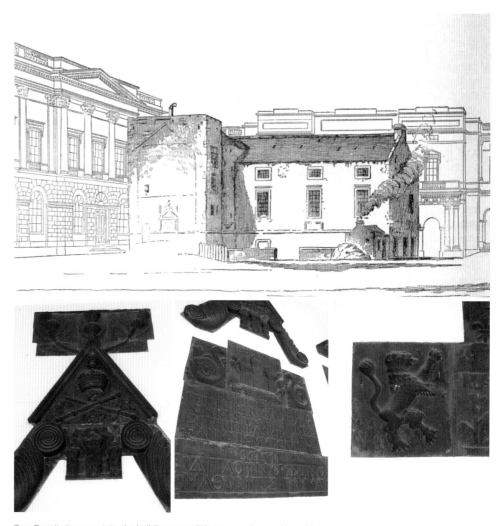

Top: Despite its poor state, the building was still in use - as the smoking chimney shows.

Bottom: Carved stones from some of the University's early buildings were preserved when the buildings were demolished; this one was from the 1617 Library.

Throughout the first half of the 17th century, there was a great deal of building activity on the Kirk o' Field site. A council visitation to look at the 'fabrick' of the college in 1614 determined that the halls used by the 'magistrands' (the final-year students) and 'bajans' (first-year students) were 'too strait' (small or narrow) for the number of students they needed to accommodate, and a building programme was therefore put in place. Most significant, perhaps, was 'the Duke's library to be built' in 1616. The 'hall and library to be built with[in] College' was to be a two-storey building, over 100 feet in length and about 30 feet broad. The lower floor was to be used as a common hall and the upper floor served as the library. During a royal visit to Edinburgh in 1617, King James pronounced himself 'godfather to the College' and gave his name to it. The town council placed a Latin inscription to this effect, and at the graduation ceremony in 1620, reference was made to the building as 'speciosas et spatiosas edes' ('a handsome and spacious building').

The building is shown in a very different light in some of the later drawings, which depict a building which looks almost derelict (as it possibly was by that time) – but again 'artistic licence' may have been used here. It is possible that these drawings were commissioned as part of the campaign to get more funds together to complete the building of Old College, and so emphasising the huge crack running down the wall may have prompted Edinburgh's citizens to dig deep into their pockets and contribute towards the costs of Old College! A few of the carved stones – including one which is visible in these drawings – were retained when the buildings were demolished all those years ago and were built into the wall of a lobby in Old College.

Archaeologists uncovered destruction deposits which can be dated to 1823 - when the 1617 building was finally demolished. These remains proved to be associated with the 1617 building itself and helped to indicate things like the internal paint scheme and decorative plasterwork. Assorted glass, ceramics and a number of bones were uncovered in association with the 1617 building.

This drawing shows the 1617 Library in a sorry state, with the new buildings developing around it.

The Teaching of Anatomy

Although our excavations were unable to go as far as the anatomy building itself, we did find evidence of anatomy teaching. In amongst the soil strewn across the site were many fragments of human bone. Some of these are clearly part of earlier burials and nothing to do with the University, but the bones collected around the 1617 building were of particular interest as they included human remains which may not have originated from the cemetery. Two fragments of tibia and two pieces of cranium have all been neatly cut through by a saw. It is known that the anatomy theatre was at the southern end of the 1617 building, and it seems we have found the handiwork of an anatomy student.

Saw-marks on bone fragments may be the work of anatomy students.

Old College was built on the site of a medieval graveyard, and because the site originally sloped quite steeply from north-west to south-east, a lot of work seems to have been done before Old College was built to create a reasonably level site for the new building. This means that there is a lot of older material mixed in with newer material – fragments of human and animal bone, stone and plaster fragments from older buildings as they were demolished, charcoal from old hearths – all of which made the site very difficult to interpret.

We could not excavate the anatomy building itself - for the simple reason that it now lies underneath the main archway entrance to Old College! The development of the University is linked closely with the development of Edinburgh as a city, and as the New Town started to develop in the 18th century, plans were drawn up for a link between New Town and Old Town. North Bridge was built, and then work started on South Bridge in 1786, with plans for a grand entry into the city from London and the south. This involved realigning existing roads, and the college's premises were truncated to allow for the new roadway. South Bridge cut through the area, leaving what used to be the College Garden and the Principal's Garden to the east of the new road, and the remainder of the college premises to the west of the new road. As the sciences developed and as Edinburgh became a world-leading medical school, anatomy was obviously of great importance as a subject. But the teaching of anatomy was not without its difficulties. In times of greater religious observance but much ignorance about many things and a strong belief in superstition – King James VI, during whose reign the University was founded, was a firm believer in witchcraft – dissection of bodies was an activity many people viewed with suspicion.

Class cards issued to students showed that they had paid their fees and were entitled to attend.

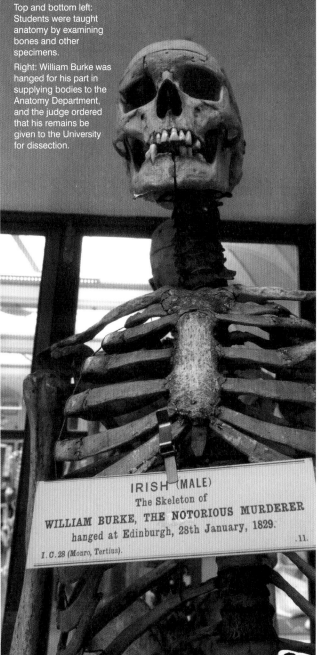

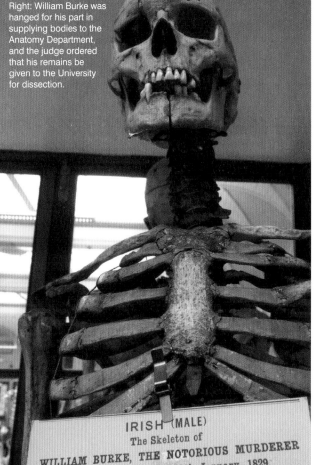

Top and bottom left: Students were taught anatomy by examining bones and other specimens.

Right: William Burke was hanged for his part in supplying bodies to the Anatomy Department, and the judge ordered that his remains be given to the University for dissection.

IRISH (MALE)
The Skeleton of
WILLIAM BURKE, THE NOTORIOUS MURDERER
hanged at Edinburgh, 28th January, 1829.
I.C.28 (Monro, Tertius). .11.

It must also have been a particularly unpleasant task in the days before refrigeration, and although space in the college buildings was often at a premium, professors in other subjects were not willing to share their teaching space with the anatomists. The anatomy building was therefore almost detached from the other buildings, presumably because the practice was viewed with distaste by many. Dr Alexander Munro petitioned for a new 'anatomical theatre' to be built for him in 1764. He ended up funding it himself – at a cost of £300 – but was reimbursed over a period of time by the College treasurer.

We know quite a lot about how anatomy was taught – from Edinburgh's records and from elsewhere. The supply of cadavers for dissection was limited, and so the practice was for the professor to carry out the dissection, with the students looking on from rows of seats – hence the description of this as a 'theatre'. A marble slab took centre stage, with the professor demonstrating to the class. Students got little hands-on experience, though they were able to examine specimens of body parts which were pickled and stored in glass jars. A particularly unpleasant part of Edinburgh's history involves the notorious body-snatchers, Burke and Hare. William Burke and William Hare were Irish labourers who arrived in Edinburgh in 1828 – by which time Old College was well under construction – to work on the Union Canal. They soon found that they could earn more money from digging up bodies and supplying them to the anatomists, and then that the earnings were even easier if they murdered people and delivered those bodies instead. It is believed that they murdered 16 people before being brought to justice. Recent discovery of a tunnel under Chambers Street to deliver bodies to the college bears out the theory that much of this work was being done with some secrecy.

The Principal's House – and a Murder Mystery

One of the most exciting historic events to have happened at the south corner of the quad was the murder of Lord Darnley, second husband to Mary, Queen of Scots. This of course happened before the University was founded. Lord Darnley was visiting the Queen but was not allowed to stay with her as he was recovering from a nasty bug. Things were not all perfect in the royal household and it seems that it was time for Darnley to be removed. During one night in 1567, there was a huge explosion and the place where Darnley was staying was blown up. Darnley was killed - we know now that he was actually strangled rather than being killed in the explosion.

Left: This contemporary drawing depicts the scene in 1567 when the prebendaries' lodgings were blown up and Lord Darnley was killed.

Below: Mary, Queen of Scots.

Although the layout isn't correct in this old drawing, you can clearly see a lot of rubble. This was the remains of the Prebendaries Lodgings, the grand building where Darnley would stay the night when not allowed at the Palace of Holyrood. Of special interest in this sketch is that immediately adjacent to the destroyed building was the Provost's lodging, which was built around 1512 and was three storeys high. The crow-stepped gables and the stair-tower are typical for that date. That house was adapted in 1583 to be part of the University and provide accommodation for the Principal; and it was eventually demolished in 1818 to make way for Old College – so the site of Darnley's murder is now largely under the Old College buildings.

In 1648, Principal Adamson had to vacate the house due to its poor condition. Whether it was rebuilt or simply repaired, a building on that site remained in use for many years as the Principal's residence, with a new kitchen being added in 1664 and a new wing being added in 1698. Daniel Defoe, author of Robinson Crusoe, visited Edinburgh in 1807. He was quite rude about most of the University's buildings, but reported that the Principal had 'a very handsome dwelling-house and garden in the College'.

The Kirk o' Field

Completing our circuit of the quadrangle, in the south-west corner of the site, we hoped the excavations would uncover evidence of a building which predated the foundation of the college. There was not a great deal to see, however – Kirk o' Field had been built on slightly raised ground, and when the site was later prepared for the building of Old College, it would appear that anything that remained of the Kirk was swept away to level the site. In this corner, the archaeologists were quickly down to the bedrock. Additionally, re-use of stone for other buildings obviously made sense, especially at a time when transport was difficult, and archaeologists often refer to a site having been 'quarried' in order to create a new building. We may think of a quarry as a site where natural rock is being excavated, but on many urban sites, such as this one, 'quarrying' involved the re-use of materials from older buildings which were no longer required. In areas of previous Roman occupation, for example, it can be common to find a Latin inscription built into the wall of a barn – upside down, perhaps – as a cost-conscious farmer has 'recycled' building material for his own purposes.

Kirk o' Field had once been a sizeable church, but by the time of these drawings was just a ruin. The city gate is to the right.

The Kirk o' Field church was probably founded early in the 12th century. Going under various names, but often referred to as the Church of St Mary in the Fields, the building originally stood just outside the city walls (hence 'in the Fields'), though the walls were later realigned. In the early 1500s, the establishment became a collegiate church – nothing to do with the 'college' as such, but a reference to the fact that a community of priests and prebendaries (rather than one single priest) had responsibility for offering masses and prayers.

The burgh council had had its eyes on the Kirk o' Field site for some years, putting forward proposals in 1562 to improve charitable provision for the poor and arrange education for the young by taking over the site for a 'scule'. The taint of Darnley's murder seems to have added impetus to the proposed transfer of the property to the council, and the 'great lodging' and other buildings were forfeited.

A modern anatomy department can do much to work out what people look like from skulls and using facial reconstructions. For someone famous like Lord Darnley, many portraits exist, but they were flattering compared to reality. What is perhaps surprising is that the supposed skull of Darnley was located in the collections in our Anatomy Museum long before the dig took place. As you can see from the image, it is a little broken but this happened later as the inscription written directly on the skull has a part missing.

The inscription says "Skull of Lord Darn(ley) found in Kirk o Field in College Square Edin'r." Bracketed letters are on the broken piece. We now know that the reason a piece was removed from Darnley's skull was to test whether he had suffered from syphilis. The verdict was that he had not. It seems likely that the skull was given to anatomy by Dr Paterson who was a graduate of the Medical School at University of Edinburgh. He spent much of his career at Bridge of Allan and had close associations with royalty as Queen Victoria spent time in the area, and he met her on several occasions. Paterson was a great collector of unusual objects and research shows that his collection included the skull of Darnley.

Early on in this book, we noted that an archaeological dig sometimes fails to find anything, and sadly that was largely the case with this area of the quad. We know quite a lot about Kirk o' Field because it was a significant building in its own right, and because it was the site of an infamous and high profile murder. But in terms of what was found, this section was disappointing. The main finds were a network of drains, dating from late Victorian times or possibly even early 20th century – and the site of some 20th century bike stands! The maroon-glazed drainage pipes were made in Cumbernauld.

Even with little finds like this, we learn something – and the holes left by the bicycle stands demonstrate how human activity leaves a footprint in the earth, however modest the building activity might have been.

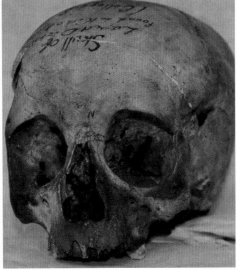

Top and bottom left: In 1612, the town council offered to 'put up a great gate'.

Bottom right: This skull in the University's Anatomy Museum is reputed to be that of Lord Darnley.

History Unveiled

So far, this book has walked you around the quad and looked at each building in turn. In terms of the University's history, this gives a pretty confusing picture, so at this point it might be helpful to explain how the site developed chronologically.

The first building on the site, before the foundation of the University, was Kirk o' Field and the associated prebendaries' lodgings. Prebendaries were priests who shared the duties in what was, at the time, a large and important church – and just as monks live in monasteries, prebendaries had residential accommodation adjacent to the church. At the time of the University's foundation, the buildings comprised 'the yarde, chambers, and lodging, and kirk, belonging to the collegial provestry and prebendaries of the Kirk-a-field'. The Provost's Lodgings were used as a residence for the early Principals of the University. The prebendaries' lodgings were just a pile of rubble by this time, following the explosion in 1567. Stone from them – and from other redundant buildings - was almost certainly recycled into later buildings for the new college.

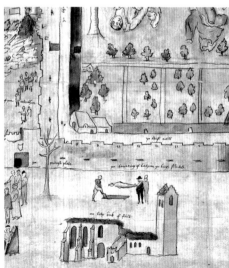

Next came Hamilton House, former home of James Hamilton, Duke of Chatelherault and 2nd Duke of Arran and built around 1562. This domestic building became the first home of the University in 1583. One early piece of essential equipment was purchased – on 6 December 1583, an order was made to 'buy a Bell and hang it upon the College'. This bell was in fact made from two old bells melted down to make one new bell, in an early move towards recycling – but with the students' day starting as early as 5 a.m., a bell must indeed have been an essential item.

In 1587, houses, a yard and a wynd belonging to Mr James Richie at Kirk o' Field were purchased for the college. In 1612 the town council offered to 'put up a great gate', and there are various references to the gate over the years, though no archaeological evidence for it.

Cramped premises led to a building programme, and in 1617 the 'Duke's Library' was added.

Houses adjacent to the college were purchased in 1634 to allow the college to be enlarged, and over the next few years a lot of tidying up was done – old thatched houses were demolished, ruinous houses were 'enclosed with a Wall being unseemly to behold', and so on.

The whole campus must have been a building site for some years, though improvements were made – a sundial was installed in November 1638 and repairs were ordered to the built-in desks in the Great Auditory or main hall. Skeen's Lodging near the High School (not far from the Old College site) was bought in 1641 and became the dwelling for the professor of divinity. In 1642, the 'new library' was built, and the college had its own printing house too.

Much adaptation and updating of buildings – including the latrines – seems to have gone on from this point; a museum was created in a 'closet' in 1695, a house was built for the gardeners in 1702, and the council ordered that the steeple should be finished in 1705.

Professor John Walker taught natural history in the building below.

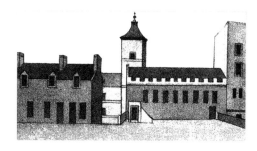

During the 18th century, there were a few developments, perhaps the most significant of which was the building of an 'anatomical theatre'.

Robert Adam was then commissioned to design a new building, and drew up plans for a double quadrangle. Playfair's later design of a single quadrangle is what was actually built. In 1789, the foundation stone was laid for Old College, and work started to replace the muddle of buildings with a single edifice worthy of the growing University.

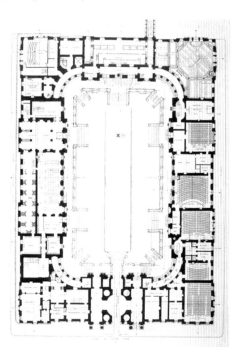

Drains, Drains and More Drains

We take so many things for granted. We go home, switch on the light, turn up the central heating, take the soup out of the fridge, and heat it in the microwave. We wash up afterwards, without a thought as to where the water comes from or where the waste water goes to. Life in the quad buildings was very different. We've already heard about the 'moustyness' in the Library which led to an order for extra coals for the fires, and in 1626 the library's Keeper was instructed to hire a servant to light the building and air the books. With every classroom warmed by a coal fire – as well as every house in the city cooking on fires – 'Auld Reekie' will certainly have earned its name. But in addition to storage space for coals, provision had to be made for water supplies, and for removal of waste.

In the early years, water for the college came from various wells on the site, which had to be cleaned and repaired regularly. No trace of these was found during the excavations. What we did find, however, were numerous drains which had been put in place since the 1790s. Many of these cut through earlier archaeological remains or the skeletal remains which were discovered during the excavation.

There were many problems with the 'latterns' or latrines. A 'filthy puddle' making its way under the boundary wall of the college precinct caused damage to neighbouring property, and from council records it seems to have taken at least six years to get that matter resolved! The old latrines were replaced in 1649 with a row of new ones, but problems continued, with a committee discussing 'how the college may be kept free of the fifth to be brought out of the Latterns'. Eventually, in 1749, there was an order 'for building a New House of office for the College' – new latrines, in other words. Whether or not this solved the problem is not clear.

In 1729, the college was ordered to make a 'syver' – a drain – from 'the Back of the Poultry Market to Marlins Wynd', and a few years later in 1738, there was an order for a well and gutter-stones to be laid on the south side of the library.

Edinburgh was one of the first towns to have water piped to buildings, and water was brought in hollowed-out elm logs from as far away as Harlaw in the Pentland Hills. In 1741, the Principal and professors were allowed to install a branch pipe from Potterrow – at a cost of £15 – to buildings in the quadrangle, and permission was also given to demolish a 'draw well'. Presumably, with the modern technology of piped water, a well was seen as hopelessly old-fashioned. But there was still a well for the use of the 'Cold Bath' and for use by the inhabitants of the college.

Other developments to the infrastructure followed, with a street 'from the College Gate to Dr Black's class' being paved in 1776.

Plans from Victorian times show ducts for 'vitiated air', an early form of health and safety provision. This is air which is deprived of oxygen and low in oxygen content. In the early days of the buildings, coal fires and candles in crowded rooms would have resulted in the air becoming contaminated - not just with carbon dioxide from people breathing out but also with carbon monoxide from the fires and lights. Conditions must have been very unpleasant – especially when you add in the smells from the medical lecture theatres and dissection rooms. It was some years before people knew the difference between carbon dioxide and carbon monoxide, but ducting for 'vitiated air' was probably an early form of ventilation, designed to carry contaminated air from inside the building out to the quad. Work on deaths caused from mining and working inside railway tunnels led to better understanding of these issues.

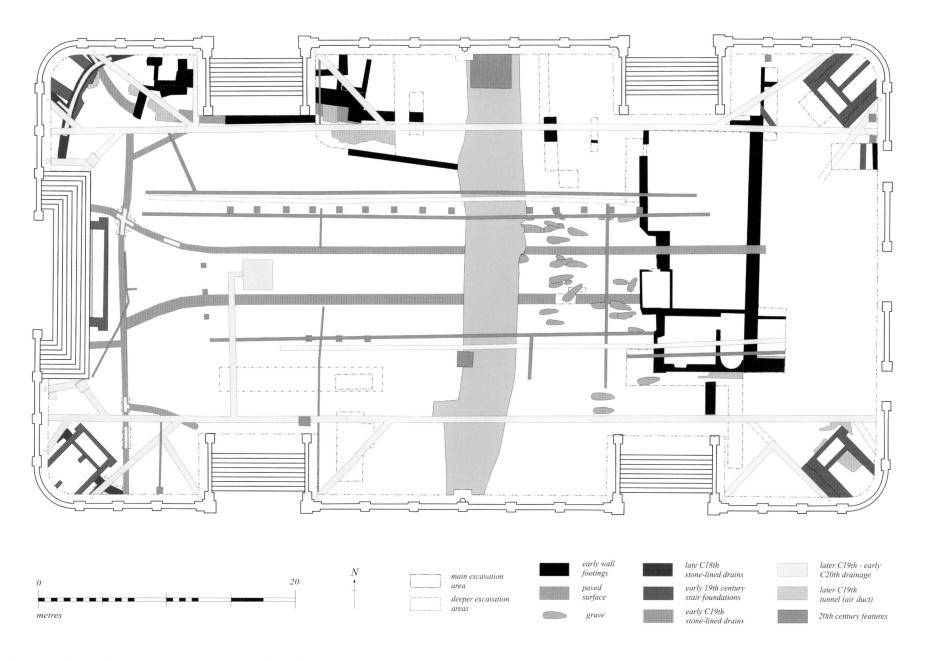

early wall
footings

paved
surface

grave

early C19th
stone-lined drains

late C18th
stone-lined drains

early 19th century
stair foundations

later C19th - early
C20th drainage

later C19th
tunnel (air duct)

20th century features

main excavation
area

deeper excavation
areas

N

0   20

metres

Plan showing the variety of surfaces uncovered - and the extent to which this site had been reworked over the years.

Chemistry in Action

The archaeological dig was almost complete - the new slabs and grass were ready to lay and our glimpse into the past was about to be covered over. However, just at the last minute it was suggested that perhaps more material relating to chemistry might be hidden within the library store. Being an institution of learning we could not miss the opportunity to find out more about our past, particularly in the sciences at this period of history. So funds were rapidly raised and a two week extension enabled a deeper investigation under the library. The outcomes were stunning.

Hazardous chemicals meant the archaeologists needed full protective clothing.

The wide variety of vessels is evidence of the broad range of experimentation which was being carried out. Some (such as the blue and white bowl) clearly have domestic origins, while we know that others were specially commissioned from Josiah Wedgwood's factory.

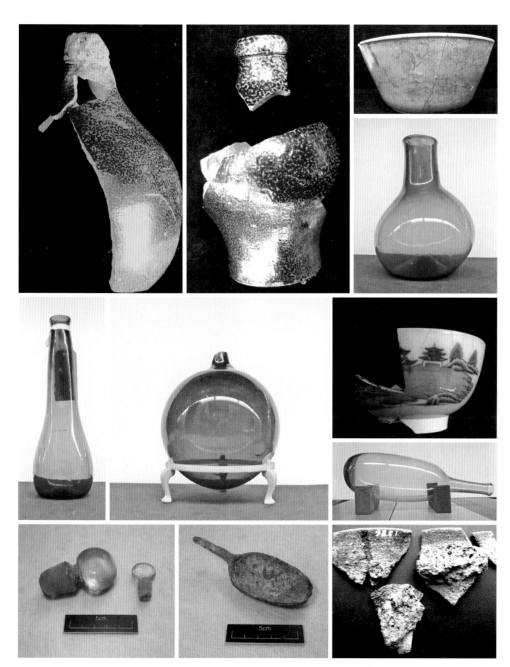

We discovered artefacts from the time when Joseph Black and his colleagues were doing experiments and melting things in crucibles. We found glass and ceramic fragments. These were obviously parts of retorts and condensing chambers. Some even had residues of chemicals in them. Excavation of the cellars under the 1642 library led to the discovery of some very interesting finds.

Brightly coloured compounds were uncovered and sent for analysis - the results concluded that the red solid contained mercury and the pink solid contained arsenic and cobalt. All of these are highly toxic even after years in the ground, which made the excavation difficult. The compounds were found adjacent to chemistry apparatus, which helped to explain their presence. We know that the chemistry department of the University was located to the rear of the 1642 building from 1781 to 1820 within Printing House Yard and that Thomas Charles Hope, who succeeded Joseph Black as Professor of Chemistry stored Black's old chemical apparatus in the basement of the 1642 building. It is thus very possible that the chemistry equipment and materials recovered in this trench relate to Black's own laboratory!

A second fascinating aspect of this was where these items of equipment were being developed. New tools were needed for this new science of chemistry and it seems that Josiah Wedgwood, the famous potter, was producing experimental vessels for Joseph Black, and a glass maker in Leith was producing the glass. Chemists today are so lucky to just go to the catalogue and select what they need. It is remarkable how well connected these innovators and entrepreneurs of the time were, but also how much effort they had to put into designing and obtaining the equipment they needed.

Joseph Black did not research alone, and there were many other colleagues and notable students. Indeed, Charles Darwin himself found the lectures in chemistry and pharmacy exciting, in contrast to his lectures in medicine, which he found tedious.

The University as an Institution

This book has concentrated on the physical presence of the University in the city, but a university is much more than simply its buildings. Starting off with just a handful of boys learning Latin, Greek grammar, logic, rhetoric and arithmetic – in preparation for life in the Church for many of them – the University increased its student numbers and its range of subjects over the years. At the outset, one master or 'regent' took a cohort of boys through their studies for the whole of their four years at the Tounis College – there was no specialist teaching in any subject. Studies were interrupted from time to time by outbreaks of the plague, when the entire University decamped to Linlithgow for up to a year at a time, or classes were simply dismissed.

The early students came from within Edinburgh and Leith, and from across Scotland. Most of them were around 12-14 years old, and the college was therefore more a 'school' than what we would now think of as a university. Students paid tuition fees direct to the regent. Although there were some attempts to make Edinburgh a residential university – like the Oxford and Cambridge colleges – adequate student accommodation was never built and so boys either lived with their families or took lodgings with regents or with landlords in town. This led to some bad behaviour, with many notes of windows being broken, criticism of students favouring billiards over study, students being fined for being seen in taverns, and so on.

Despite a long teaching day – starting as early as 5am – students found time for games, as these doodles by Archibald Flint in the margins of his notebook show.

Student numbers had increased over the first 100 years of the college, but then dropped significantly in the 1690s when fashionable people chose to send their sons abroad for a modern education. At Leiden and Utrecht, for example, students could be educated in languages, fine arts and music. In response to this, the town council decided to overhaul the University's curriculum, and between 1703 and 1726 the college adopted a new system, replacing the regents with professors who took responsibility for specialist subjects. This radical approach attracted students from England too.

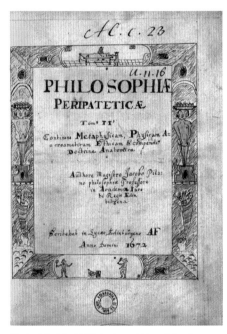

Student Archibald Flint adorned his notebook with wishful pictures of how he'd like to be spending his time.

The eighteenth century must have been an exciting time in Edinburgh. In addition to the burgeoning University – by 1750 there were about 650 students - the College of Physicians, the Faculty of Advocates and the Surgeons Incorporation were all working to develop professional education. The New Town was being built, plans for a grand entry to the city from the south were being developed and eventually led to the creation of South Bridge and North Bridge - and plans were also afoot to replace the scruffy old buildings of the University.

The measured form of Old College gradually replaced the hotch-potch of buildings which had been the University's home for its first 200 years, and though the work proceeded in fits and starts, with changes of architect and changes of plan along the way, the overall impression today is of a well-designed and unified building. But look closely, and we can see that the windows on one side of the quad are quite different from the other side, that the details around the arches don't match some of those early drawings, that the clock tower drawn by Adam does not appear in later drawings and that a large dome has been added more recently. The changes of style reveal this as a building which has evolved.

Adam's original scheme for Old College included a clock tower which was never built.

A view of Old College before the dome was added.

By 1900, a large drinking fountain had been installed.

Where Are They Now?

We don't know how many boys enrolled in 1583 when the Tounis College opened, but the numbers graduating most years in the early years were around 20-30. Within a few years, the University had around 300 students. It now has over 35,000! Women weren't admitted to study until late in the 19th century, but over half of our students today are female.

Old College currently houses some of the central administration departments plus the School of Law, but the other subjects have all moved to different locations across the city. From the early 18th century, teaching of botany was carried out at the Botanical Gardens on Inverleith Row, and Astronomy used the observatory on Calton Hill.

In the 19th century, creation of the 'New Buildings' – the Medical School complex and the McEwan Hall adjacent to Middle Meadow Walk – signalled the first major expansion and positioned Edinburgh as one of the world's leading medical schools.

In the early 20th century, the purchase of a green-field site allowed the sciences to move to what is now the King's Buildings campus – with Chemistry being the first discipline to move there to what is fittingly named the Joseph Black Building.

Image Key

1. Botany was taught at the Botanical Gardens.
2. The 'New Buildings' - the Medical School - were built in the 1880s.
3. The McEwan Hall, around 1900.
4. The Joseph Black Building around 1948.
5. The Noreen and Kenneth Murray Library.
6. New College (Divinity) merged with the University in 1935.
7. The Royal (Dick) School of Veterinary Studies moved to its new home in 2011.
8. The Main Library in George Square.
9. The social sciences disciplines are grouped around George Square.
10. Pollock Halls provide residential accommodation for many students, particularly those in their first year of study.
11. Moray House, built in 1618, is the University's oldest extant building.
12. Edinburgh College of Art.
13. The University shares premises with the new Royal Infirmary at Little France.
14. Medical teaching takes place across the city, including the Western General Hospital.

New College, which started life as a separate college of divinity, merged with the University in 1935, becoming the University's Faculty of Divinity.

The Veterinary College, founded in 1823, and now affectionately known as the Dick Vet, was incorporated into the University in 1951 and recently moved to new premises at Easter Bush.

In the 1960s around George Square, a huge new library, the David Hume Tower, buildings for various social science disciplines, and a student centre to complement the Students' Union Building in Teviot House were all developed.

Purpose-built residential accommodation was established at the Pollock Halls complex in the 1970s.

Moray House School of Education merged with the University in 1998, and Edinburgh College of Art merged in 2010.

More recently, medical teaching has moved from the 'New Buildings' to the New Royal Infirmary at Little France, though students are also located in many hospitals across the city – and indeed, across Scotland. We have expanded well beyond our original home.

The University is still very much 'the town's college', concentrated across the city at various sites, but Old College – about which we now know so much more as a result of the excavations – remains at its centre and represents its true foundation.

33

Acknowledgments

Old College Quadrangle.

Just like the archaeological dig itself, producing a book always involves many people. Input from Addyman Archaeology – in particular, from Tom Addyman and Liz Jones – has been vital in helping us to interpret the complexities of this site. Two students also made an important contribution - Shannon Campbell checked various archaeological details, and Ioanna Melina Tsiknaki worked through the huge number of photographs and historical illustrations to link the text to the pictures.

Published by the University of Edinburgh Communications and Public Affairs

Printed by J Thomson Colour Printers.

Designed by www.hamlindaniels.co.uk

www.ed.ac.uk

The illustrations in this book come from various sources, and we are grateful for permission to reproduce them here. The photographs of the dig in progress, the various diagrams, and the images of finds, were supplied by Addyman Archaeology. Images of objects in the National Museum of Scotland's Playfair Collection on page 29 are by K Robin Murdoch. The majority of the other photographs were supplied by the University of Edinburgh. Historical illustrations are reproduced from those sources, or from material owned by the authors. Every effort has been made to trace copyright holders, but if any have been inadvertently overlooked, the publisher will be pleased to make the necessary arrangement at the first opportunity.